The Book Marketing Plan

How To Market a Book In a Brave New World

By Dan Moskel

Dan Moskel

Copyright © 2014 Dan Moskel
All Rights Reserved.

www.danmoskeluniversity.com

Reproduction or translation of any part of this work beyond that permitted by Section 107 or 108 of the 1976 United States Copyright Act without permission of the copyright owner is unlawful.

This publication is designed to provide accurate and authoritative information in regard to the subject matter covered. It is sold with the understanding that the publisher and author is not engaged in rendering legal, accounting, or other professional services. If legal advice or other expert assistance is required, the services of a competent professional person should be sought out.

ISBN-13: 978-1503322912

Printed In The United States of America

Table of Contents

Chapter 1.	The City Made of Gold	pg. 7
Chapter 2.	The Art of Persuasion	pg. 13
Chapter 3.	Be The Best	pg. 21
Chapter 4.	Be Popular	pg. 31
Chapter 5.	YouTube Videos	pg. 39
Chapter 6.	Building Your Fan Club	pg. 55
Chapter 7.	Articles	pg. 63
Chapter 8.	Social Media	pg. 69

Chapter 9.	Play With The Other Kids	pg. 73
Chapter 10.	Advertising	pg. 83
Chapter 11.	Be Omnipresent	pg. 93
Chapter 12.	Automatic Sales Funnels	pg. 101
Chapter 13.	KDP Select Promotions	pg. 111
Chapter 14.	Media Interviews	pg. 119
Chapter 15.	The Disney Lesson	pg. 125
Chapter 16.	Story Telling	pg. 131
Chapter 17.	Maximum ROI	pg. 135

| Chapter 18. | Change The World | pg. 143 |
| Chapter 19. | Free Gift From The Author | pg. 147 |

Other Books by Dan Moskel

Online Marketing - The Shark Attack

How To Write a Book - The System

Video Marketing For Entrepreneurs

The Blueprint To Affiliate Marketing

The Magical Message of Success

How To Create a Website: Easy Button

Email Marketing That Works ... So You Don't Have To

Entrepreneur Bible To Riches

SEO Training Manual - The 10 Golden Steps To Shower In Search Engine Traffic

The Book Marketing Plan

Chapter 1. The City Made of Gold

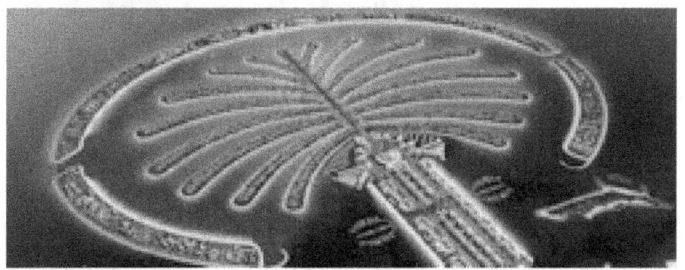

Once upon a time there was a city made of gold. Every day the people of this city we're building magnificent architecture, skyscrapers, and wonders of our modern world.

One day this city could boast of the only seven star hotel, host the annual richest horse race in the world, the tallest building, and even a man made island, that can be seen from outer space.

Because of this celebrities would flock from all over the world to visit, and the New York Times published an article saying: *"Dubai has become the kind of city where you might run into Michael Jordan at the Buddha Bar or stumble across Naomi Campbell celebrating her birthday with a multi day bash."*

Because of that, the most sought after, wealthiest, and best customers in the world, including more celebrities such as Kobe Bryant, Tom Cruise, David Beckham, Giorgio Armani, and many more. Would travel from far and distant lands to bring their gold to this city.

Until finally, the city of Dubai, was featured in a Rory McIlroy and Omega watch commercial, with the soundtrack of Hall of Fame, by The Script, and featuring will.i.am.

The first reason I share this story with you, is not because we were recently interviewed for a TV show in Dubai. Instead, it's to point out that you too can build a group of customers, fans, and people eagerly seeking you out to give you their gold. Just like the great city of Dubai.

Next, look at everything this city has done to attract the wealthiest customers in the world.

You see, the big piles of gold for every author, aren't simply in the few dollars in book royalties. Instead, it's in providing more value to the market in the form of speaking engagements, coaching, writing more books, consulting, selling products and services, the sky's the limit.

There's three parts to this book, in the first we'll discuss the foundation of effective marketing. Along with making your book attractive to the wealthiest customers in the world.

In the second part, we go step by step through the six automatic sales funnels. This includes: YouTube videos, social media, articles, email marketing, building your fan club, distribution avenues, and much more.

This is how we manufacture the Oprah effect for your book. And guarantee that you've got royalty payments hitting your bank account, as often as LeBron James makes jump shots.

In the third and final section, we discuss advanced marketing strategies, and dive deep into how exactly to earn maximum ROI, return on investment, from your book.

Now, I've been working with marketing full time since 2006, and have earned millions of dollars. You may have even seen me on national TV in my own commercial, appearing on ESPN, NatGeo, Comedy Central, MTV, VH-1, A&E, and many more.

I only share this with you, so you know, we ain't blowing hot air over here. Marketing is my trade, skill, and life's work.

Warning

Yes, a warning this is not a book for wantreprenuers, excuse makers, or those desperate to just think positively and have checks magically appear in the mailbox.

This is a blunt revelation of how exactly to make your book become a best seller.

And as the late great Earn Nightingale said our rewards in life are in direct proportion to the amount of service we provide. In this spirit we've created a number of bonus gifts for you. The first includes a training course with videos, were you'll get a behind the scenes look at precisely how to deploy these book marketing weapons.

And for the first 100 people that sign up at DanMoskelUniversity.com, and join our congregation. We've created two extra special bonuses with a retail value of $197.00. This includes personal one on one help with me, full details inside.

Dan Moskel

Chapter 2. The Art of Persuasion

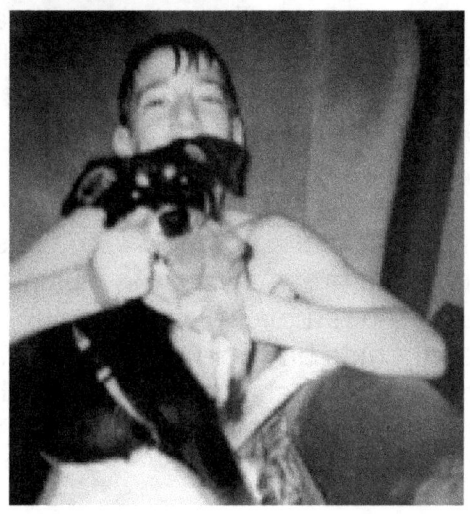

Now, it's no debate persuasive writing exists. And when you really boil it down, kids, and dogs are the most persuasive, and thus the best salesmen!

Heck, my dog Licky, she could just "look" pitiful, any time there was food around, and she was rewarded generously for this effective selling technique.

Specifically we're looking at your book description page, at online retailers. It may be obvious, that you need to write a compelling description, but this is the #1 mistake we see with the authors, we speak to.

You see, we've got to convince, persuade, and sell people that your book, is the best available and a great value, with multiple benefits for the reader. This is how we persuade them to buy your book, and if we can't do this effectively it doesn't matter how many people know about your book, ain't nobody going to be buying it.

In the world of marketing, persuasive writing is called copywriting. This is the special sauce, and the exact, precise words, that persuade people to give you their gold for your book.

The plain truth is most people preaching about branding, couldn't sell their way out of a paper bag! And like it or not your book description is one of the few items of information a potential buyer gets to see. And thus, this information must be compelling and convince them to buy your book. It's one of the few items they'll their decision to buy or not, based upon.

It's best to approach your description, just like a sales letter. And if you are unable or unwilling to accept selling, then you'd better embrace Michael Scott, at The Office and whip up another batch of Jello to put Dwight Schrute's calculator in.

Before we go thru this in detail, it's important to note, the most effective marketing starts with the who. Who exactly is going to be giving you the money? Please, write down as much information as you can about this, your perfect, ideal, consumer including: their age, income, gender, family, hopes, dreams, fears, everything.

Doing this exercise, will help focus your message, and empower you to pop through the clutter, and really speak, and connect to your target customer. And thus, sell more copies of your book!

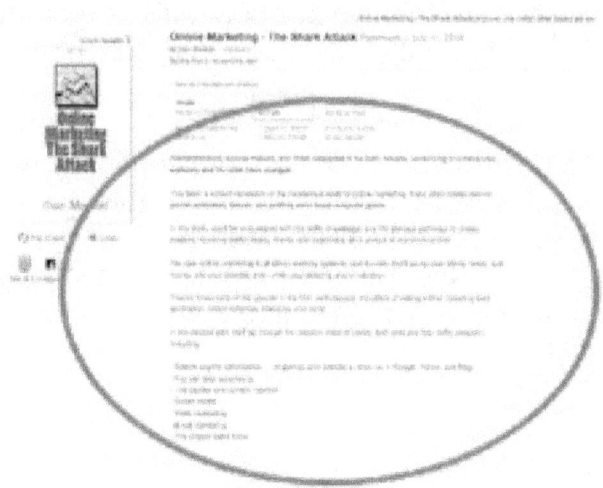

The Selling System

Now, there's a number of acronym's for the motivating sequence in a sales presentation, regardless if it's selling with the written word, face to face, over the phone, it applies to all. We're going to keep this as simple as possible, and discuss the most common one, AIDA, Attention, Interest, Desire, and Action.

1. Attention

How do you get anyone's attention? How about your kids?

You speak to them, their concerns, their wants, needs, goals, desires. And you make your words, interesting and applicable to them. The title of your book is the first place that grabs attention, but you also need to use this in the first sentences of your book description.

Be different, be unique, and pop through the clutter, so you can get his attention. And now you can dive into your sales presentation and convince him to buy your useful book.

2. Interest

The second step is to build interest. This is where we describe exactly what's in the pages of your book, and the benefits your potential reader will get with your material. In other words, how exactly will his life improve with your information?

Be specific, and look at everything through the eyes of your reader, not from your perspective. After all, your book is talking to other people, it ain't just written for you to read!

3. Desire

This is the true selling action, share with your potential reader how their life will change, and transform with your useful information. Tell them why you've got the best book in your genre, and why it's different than all the other books.

Think in terms of what they get. Why your book and how precisely it'll help them.

4. Action

This is where you ask and ask specifically for your potential reader to buy your book. Don't be fearful, and don't neglect it, we must ask for everything we want in life, from what were having for dinner, to who our spouse will be. Ask clearly, loudly, and specifically.

For more about the selling process we're conducing an upcoming live copywriting event, simply visit DanMoskelUniversity.com and sign up to attend.

Avoid trying to write a perfect description, but do invest time with this and make it compelling, persuasive, and interesting. After all, this is what your potential reader will see most often, and is a big factor in the buying decision for them.

You'll sell more books by narrowing down, and focusing your message on a specific segment of the market, and avoid trying to write a book for everyone. As Mark Cuban of the Shark Tank says: "when you're trying to please everyone, you usually please no one."

And a frequent mistake among entrepreneurs and authors, is thinking they can sell their goods, books, and widgets to anyone, and everyone. This often results in selling to no one!

It's important to be clear, be specific, and be excited. A key aspect of good selling is to get your audience, excited, eager, and in a frenzy to get your book, products, and services.

Much like the churches that practice handling snakes. And I guarantee you these do exist.

Growing up the son of a preacher man, it's natural for me to see the way formal religions use selling principles. For if convincing someone to pick up a poisonous snake, isn't selling I don't know what is.

Maybe you prefer the Orsen Wells example, with his infamous radio broadcast The War of The Worlds. In this play he convinced a huge number of Americans that aliens we're attacking from outer space, and Judgment Day was upon thee.

No joke this dramatization sent massive numbers of people out into the night in a frenzied state of panic!

By the way, Orsen Wells used the publicity that this event brought him, and was able to domino this opportunity into a career in Hollywood and made many box office hits, including Citizen Kane!

Chapter 3. Be The Best

Look, it's key that your book is the best value, in order to sell it. There's some methods to help with this, but it ultimately boils down to providing the most service to your reader.

This is how you differentiate your book from all the others within your specific genre. In the world of marketing, this is called your USP, or unique selling proposition. And you can see examples of this with the good businesses, everyday.

This is precisely why people should purchase your book, instead of your competitors. And it's much easier to sell your book, when you know it's the best value available.

Opportunity Versus Outcome

You see, your book is media, just like a YouTube video, website, and advertisement on TV. It's a way for people to discover you, and your expertise.

But, many businesses, and authors view a purchase of their goods, as an outcome. This is the forsaken path. You must view this as an opportunity to create a relationship with your reader. And an opportunity to provide more value, and more help to them, in order to maximize the gold you can earn.

The 7 Value Adding Bonuses

1. Free Reports

It's wise to provide and offer additional help. This can be in related topics, and subjects. For example, one of the ways we want to help readers of our 8th book, _How To Write a Book - The System_, is by providing a free report about how to market a book.

You see this is offering more service, value, and help. It also gives you the opportunity to build a fence around your fan club, because you should ask your reader, to visit your website and sign up for your bonus reports. This way you can continue to communicate with him, and provide value to him.

2. Training videos

Technology empowers us to provide massive value to our readers. One of the ways, you can do this is by offering training videos. As an example in our 9th book, *Online Marketing - The Shark Attack* we provide a series of training videos, to show folks how exactly to use these online media tools, and advertising platforms.

This includes a behind the scenes look at how to set up a campaign in Google AdWords, and the true nuts and bolts of how all these different media weapons, and traffic sources can be used most effectively.

3. Live events

Yes offer a free bonus live event, where of course you go about sharing your knowledge. You can obviously provide a question and answer, training events on specific subjects, and the sky's the limit. This is a great way to engage and connect with your reader, and give them more of what they want.

4. Free consultation, appointment, strategy session ...

One of the great methods to add valuable bonuses is to offer a free consultation, appointment, strategy session, custom plan, or any other personal one on one assistance to your reader.

One example is with this book and how we're also offering the first 100 people a free media interview, to increase awareness, interest people, and drive more sales for your book. And more royalties to your bank account.

Book marketing isn't rocket science, it's providing value to your reader. And our objective with this book, is to show you exactly how to domino your book, to get more sales, royalties, and great, big, piles of cold hard cash!

5. Contests

You can always run a contest and be creative with entries for a prize. For example, with one book, they offer to give away a convertible. You don't have to be this extravagant, but please do put on your thinking cap.

6. Behind the scenes

Give your readers a bonus and show them how you went about creating your book, a behind the scenes look, a backstage pass. This applies to non fiction and fiction, and it's cool to hear how an author went about crafting, and weaving their story. For I'd be very interested in learning how exactly John Grisham goes about writing his spectacular literature.

7. Interviews

One last bonus includes providing your reader, access to an interview of you. For example, you could offer your readers to view the interview we conduct together. And this simply gives your reader, more access to you, which is what they want.

The big picture goal with your bonuses, is to let people connect with you, create a relationship, and provide value, and help to them. This requires you to give them more of you, and your knowledge, expertise, and information.

Include Bonus Offers In Your Description

Once you've chosen and created some additional bonuses to offer your readers, it's wise to tell them about these extra value adding bonuses, in your description.

This'll additionally help you differentiate and separate your book, from the competing offers. It's useful to invest some time looking at what currently exists in your niche market, so you can accurately differentiate yourself. The goal is to give more, so you can earn more!

An unavoidable truth in selling is that you must build impending urgency, to get people to act, and buy your book. For we've all seen some neat, do-hickey, and have intended to purchase it.

But, we got distracted by the dinner on the stove, that's caught fire, and little Billy riding the dog again, and sticking crayons up his little sister's nose. It's essential that we get people to act, and right now.

An effective way of building this impending urgency is to offer a limited number of these bonuses. You can see an example of this with our book, <u>Online Marketing - The Shark Attack</u>, because we're offering a custom shark attack marketing plan but only for the first 250 people.

Obviously, this is a free gift and we don't earn any additional revenue. However you can see how this helps to create, build, and strengthen a relationship we have with our reader.

This urgency is key to getting them to act, and act right now, as in buy your book, this moment. Not tomorrow, not next week, but now, and we're providing them a reason to buy your book, right now.

Please, include your value adding bonuses, in the description and listing of your book. This way people know you're providing more, and the sincerity, and genuine desire to be of service, and help them, is much clearer to see.

You see, your potential reader doesn't know you, and if they feel like you really want to help them with their challenges. They'll be much more eager to buy your book, than an offer that doesn't make them feel as if there's a genuine desire to help, and provide service to them, behind it.

It's wise to both offer limited availability bonuses, along with bonus gifts for everyone that buys your book. This way you'll be creating urgency with the limited available bonuses, along with providing more service to all your readers with the bonuses for everyone.

We can't stress enough, in order to earn maximum ROI, return on investment. We must view your book sales, and your readers, as an opportunity to create a relationship together.

Not as a one night stand, or outcome, or experience. The unavoidable truth is the most challenging, and expensive path for businesses, and authors, is to find new customers. Studies reveal it's much easier approximately six times, to sell something to someone who already knows you, trusts you, and you've provided the best value too.

The fact is businesses, and authors, along with musicians, and artists, will have a group of people that love them, and want to get more from them. Now, doesn't it only seem intelligent that we should collect these folks, and give them what it is they want!

Don't worry if you're unsure of how exactly to collect this information, we'll discuss the mechanics in detail coming up. But it's mission critical that you create a list of your fans, and followers.

This list of people are the best leads in the world. It's customers. Every businesses, greatest asset is the relationship they build with their list of customers.

For Stephen King fans will be the first people running out to purchase his new book. So we ought to be the first person telling them, about his new book, and how exactly they can go and get it.

If not he's derelict in his duties, as an author, business owner, and entrepreneur. Not to mention he's not serving his fans the best, nor serving himself, or if he had stock holders.

These people, your fan club, is your best asset. They want more of you, your products, goods, services, expertise, knowledge, and want to build a relationship, of mutual benefit. You are helping everyone by leveraging this asset, and giving them what they want, which is more of you! It's a win, win, win scenario.

Chapter 4. Be Popular

Listen, a plain truth to online book retailers, such as Amazon, is they're very similar to the search engines, Google, Yahoo, and Bing. People visit online retailers and will search for keywords, in that big search bar at the top, just like they search for keywords in Google.

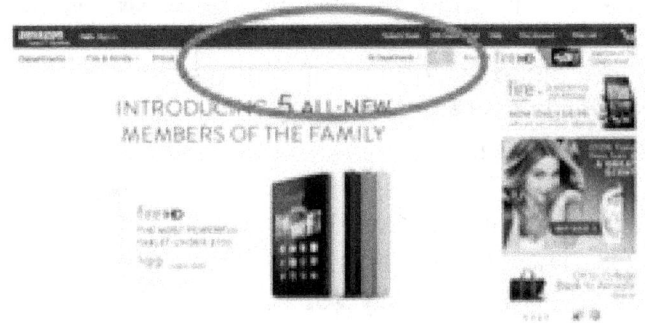

Now, the search engines use an algorithm to determine what websites, have the best information. This algorithm resembles a popularity contest, the more popular a website is, the higher it will show up when people search for those keywords.

The keyword is the exact term, and words, that people type into the search bar, and press enter to look for information about.

When it comes to being popular and having friends, and votes, these are cast with links. In other words, the website with the most votes, friends, and links to it, is considered an authority, and will rank very high in the search engines. This applies to your book as well, at online retailers.

Were going to dig into this, in full detail, with the automatic sales funnels. But here we need to first discover the specific, and exact keywords that people are looking for information about.

We can add these keywords during the publishing process to help tell the online retailers, what exactly your book is about. And the keywords you want your listing page to show up for.

It's wise to target high volume keyword terms. This ought to translate into more people seeing your book, and thus more sales, royalties, and fans for you!

Keyword Tool

The best tool, in my opinion is the Google Keyword Planner. This is a free tool, and it can be accessed using the Google AdWords platform. This is how you buy advertising with Google, and they'll give you free access to this tool.

It will provide you with the volume, and how often specific keyword terms are searched for in Google, and related keyword terms.

We want to use high volume, keyword terms. This'll help your book rank for these searches at online retailers, if you use the keyword term in your title. It's best to stick that term right at the beginning, as in the very first words.

Let's look at an example with a reader from our book, *How To Write a Book - The System*, an example right there. This reader, reached out to us, and he's in the process of writing a book, about how people can go from an employee to an entrepreneur, just as he has.

On an aside, he's running multiple successful businesses, and was originally born in Iraq. In other words he's got some real great information, that the world can benefit with.

He's using a working title of *Employee To Entrepreneur* which is fantastic, because it's clear and concise. People picking up his book, won't be confused about the information that's inside.

One thing, he can use to help increase his visibility at online retailers, and have more people view his book, is to make his title keyword rich.

Currently, the Google Keyword Planner tool, shows zero search volume for the term "*employee to entrepreneur*." However, the keyword term "*entrepreneur*" is searched for every month, over 200,000 times, and the keyword term "*entrepreneurship*" about 40,500 times, and "*how to start a business*" around 40,500 times, per month.

The Book Marketing Plan

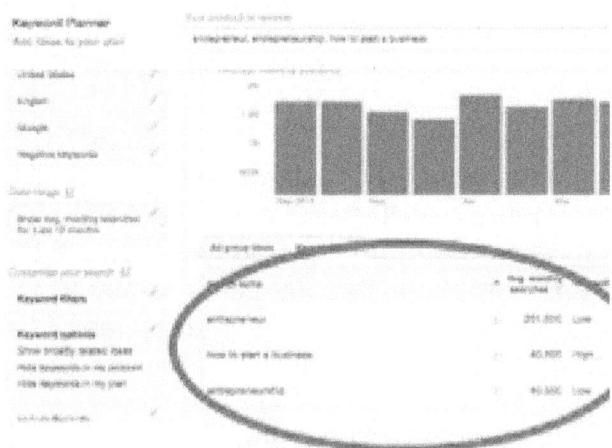

This is only the search volume for people searching with Google. We can assume there is additional volume, with Yahoo, and Bing. And don't you think it'd be safe to bet, that if there's 200,000 people searching in Google every month, for the keyword term *"entrepreneur"* there's likely a significant number of people also searching for books at Amazon, for that keyword term?

I sure do!

You see, we must take the keyword information, extrapolate it, and apply it to the online retailers. For it's not by accident there's a great, big, giant, search bar at the top of Amazon. And it only makes sense, that the same keywords people type into Google, are the same keywords they're typing into Amazon, along with Yahoo, and Bing.

Take note, because these keywords will be using again, with some of the automatic sales funnels. And I promise you the keyword tool, has been of spectacular value to me, in my career, earning great, big, giant, piles of cash, since 2006! It's very useful!

To wrap this all together, we're giving your book better odds to show up for high volume keyword terms, when people search at Amazon, if we use a keyword rich title.

For instance, a title with our example could be *The Entrepreneur Road Map - Go From Employee To Entrepreneur*, or some similar variation such as: *How To Start a Business - Transform From Employee To Entrepreneur.*

Look, this isn't a make it or break it requirement, but it can help. My philosophy is to make things as simple as possible. And Einstein would add, not simpler.

Using this can help us bring in a few more views, and sales. In addition to the automatic funnels we're going to create, momentarily.

The Book Marketing Plan

Use all the tools you can because we want to get everything working in your favor, to most efficiently get your book to be a blockbuster hit! The top priority with your title is to reach out and grab your potential readers attention!

Dan Moskel

Chapter 5. YouTube Videos

Look, here we're manufacturing your own media using YouTube videos. And we're going to use this to create the first of your automatic sales funnels.

Our big picture goal is to create videos, that get natural, organic search traffic. And then funnel those viewers to your listing page at online retailers, by including a link in the description. Along with casting a vote for you book, with this link. Thus, funneling your viewers into buyers of your book, along with improving your books popularity at the online retailers.

Hang with me, because that sounds more complicated than it is. First, I encourage you to use YouTube there are additional video marketing platforms, including Vimeo, and

MetaCafe. But if you're just starting out, let's stick with the goliath, and YouTube.

Now, before we get into the nitty gritty, of exactly what to include in your videos, it's important we share two principles. The first is we must give in order to get! In other words, you've got to make videos, that are valuable to your audience. Don't just flip on the camera, and wave your arms and tell people to go buy your book, that's not effective, and a waste of your time!

The second principle is to think in terms of your audience. Put yourself in their shoes, how would they react, respond, think, feel, about watching your video? Would you be interested in learning more, and buying your book?

If you can talk with your audience, and connect with them, along with providing valuable help to them, they're a lot more likely to go and buy your book. It's exactly like writing a book, you create it for a reader, and the audience, not for you! Please, try to look at all your marketing materials through the eyes of your audience.

The 6 Ideas For Videos

1. How To

This media gives you and everyone an easy way to demonstrate your knowledge, expertise, and authority, on your specific topic. If you show folks, how to do something and then use a call to action, that encourages them to go buy your book to learn more. They'll be a whole lot more likely to comply with your request.

2. Interviews

There's two sides to this coin. The first is you being interviewed by someone else. This can be a friend, colleague, and even someone you hire to ask you questions.

The other side includes interviewing other experts on your topic, or related information. This will make you the facilitator and will provide useful information to your audience, thus strengthening your relationship with your fans.

3. Events

YouTube enables you to conduct live events. This event can be anything, including an interview, or a training session. The goal however is to do something, fun, and interesting, and do it live.

4. Testimonials

Naturally it'll be helpful to create a few testimonials about your book, and your business. This is the story of how your information, business, products, services, helped other people, and changed their life.

5. Book Trailer

This is much like a movie preview. The idea is that you're making a video to promote your book, and drive viewers to go and get it. It's wise to view this in the same light as your book description at the online retailers.

This is your opportunity to sell your book. You've got to give folks a reason to do what it is you want, along with telling them specifically how they'll benefit by doing what you ask.

We see a lot of these videos and often it's a short video that just tells people that the creator has written a book, and the audience can go buy it. It provides no value, no reason, and there's no purpose behind it other than to promote oneself.

You can and should promote yourself, just like Donald Trump, but you've got to do this promotion the right way. For even Donald has people calling him arrogant, which is fine.

The point is there's some techniques to use self promotion, without your audience feeling as if you're promoting yourself. Just like good selling, isn't selling your goods, it's letting people know why they should buy your goods, why it's the best value available, and why it's better than all the others.

You may want to use the book trailer when you run a discount, or a Kindle countdown deal, which will be discussing in detail, coming up. But including a discount, or countdown deal, will add some urgency because it's a limited time discount price.

6. Answer Questions

Look, you'll get questions from readers of your book, and people that receive your marketing information. Answer these questions and make a video about it.

This'll significantly strengthen the relationship you have, even with people that didn't ask you that specific question. You'll be viewed as someone who truly does care, and wants to help, and thus building yourself goodwill.

Best Practices

Naturally these six ideas are merely the tip of the iceberg. You can make videos about anything, and everything. There are no rules, but do follow the YouTube guidelines to keep your account in good standing.

This is pretty basic, common sense advice, and you can access all that information at the YouTube Creator Playbook. Along with more YouTube resources that are worth looking through at your convenience.

Target Keyword Terms

Now, earlier we talked about the Google Keyword Planner tool and how this'll provide you with popular keyword terms, that people search for at Google. We extrapolated that information and applied it to people searching at Yahoo, and Bing, along with Amazon and the other online book retailers.

Once again we should take this information, and apply it to people searching at YouTube. The same idea applies, with the title of your YouTube video.

It's wise to make your video title, keyword rich, to help increase the likelihood it'll show up for these high volume keyword terms, people are searching for at YouTube. The title of your video is exactly like the title of your book, and should be approached as the headline.

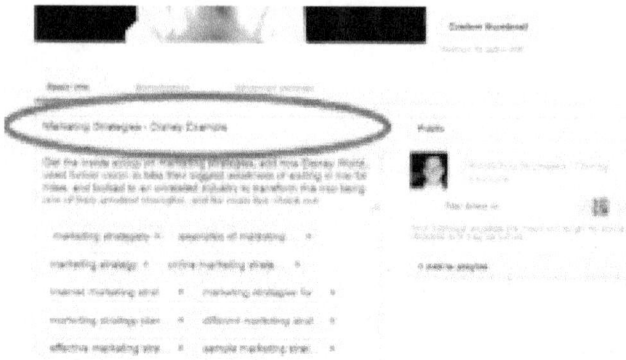

It must get attention. And I'm sure you've seen we can leverage your video to show up for keyword searches at the big three search engines. Along with YouTube searches. This is the key to getting more views for your videos.

There's two more keys we must share with you. The first is to take the exact keyword term you're targeting with your video, and include that in the tags section when you upload your video. Along with the other high volume, related keyword terms that the Google Keyword Planner provides you.

This'll help your video show up for keyword searches, and tell YouTube exactly what your video is about.

It's also very smart to write a compelling description of your video. This information will appear, next to your video in the YouTube, and search engine results. It's a way to help convince people to click, and view your video.

The second key is to include a link to your book at the online retailers in the video description. This will increase the popularity of your book at online retailers. It also makes it easy for your viewers, to go and do what you're asking of them, as in buy your book.

We'd be remiss if we didn't mention, to include a link to your website, in the video description. If you don't have a website, we're going to show you how you can create one, very affordably, and easily, and without learning computer geek code, in an upcoming chapter.

The popularity contest idea is the same with your book, as it is with your website. And by including a link from the video over to your website, and specific pages on your site. You'll be improving your website's popularity. Because that video will be casting a vote, and be seen as friend to your website.

This also applies when you make additional videos. For instance if you've made six videos, include a link from one video to another, because this will help you viewers, watch more of your material. And it'll be viewed as a vote, for the video, you're linking to.

The more votes, the better for all your online properties. Please, do avoid linking to irrelevant information. For example, if you've got a video about the best chocolate chip cookie recipes, it wouldn't make sense to link from that video to another YouTube video, containing marketing strategies, or a webpage, or a book for that matter.

The goal of the search engines is to be like a human being, so do practice some reasonable common sense. Don't stress the details or become overwhelmed, we're more than happy to show you precisely, and exactly how to go about all these steps. And if you want to know more you can grab a copy of our book, _Video Marketing For Entrepreneurs_, available at iTunes, Barnes and Noble, Amazon, and in audio book.

Video Length

Obviously the length of your videos should vary. People want information in different formats and lengths. With that said for your videos targeting keywords, it's good to keep it relatively short such as three to five minutes. This is what churches encourage to their members when they create testimony.

And for the uninitiated religious testimony is a sales presentation, and in the form of a customer testimonial. It's when people tell you how much better life is with God, regardless of which particular God they believe in.

Of course for live events, it'd be smart to give your audience more than three to five minutes. The exact amount of time for these, and any videos you make, are all up to you. I'd suggest live events be anywhere from 20 minutes to one hour.

The Formula

Now as we shared earlier with AIDA, Attention, Interest, Desire, and Action, this being the formula to sell your book. This should also be applied to your video content. You've got to get your viewers attention for them to actually watch your video, and this should be done with a hook.

Your hook, should summarize what you'll be discussing in the video and provide the reason why your viewer should watch. The interest and desire is the message you're sharing with the audience. For example, the best chocolate chip cookie recipes.

The action, is your call to action. Please, give your audience multiple reasons to respond. As in don't just ask them to buy your book, do that, but also ask them to subscribe to your channel, and visit your website, to sign up for a free report, or something they see as valuable. And give them reasons to comply with your requests.

This way you can build your fan base, and continue to follow up and communicate with these folks. Just because they didn't buy your book, right this moment, doesn't mean they won't next week, when they get paid. But you'd better remind them that your book exists next week, so they can buy.

Our top priority is to create and build relationships, just like with dating. The amount of interest, money, and respect your fan base gives you, will grow and be a consequence of what you give them.

Communicate

Look, this is common sense but please, have fun, have energy, and SMILE! Positive, optimistic, and interesting people are what others, including myself, are attracted too!

To clarify if you're making videos, and you're mumbling, and avoiding eye contact, with slumped over shoulders. They're ain't going to be many people running off to buy your book, nor connecting with you, nor wanting to have a relationship with you!

Look at kids and dogs, their excitement, and enthusiasm is infectious. And this is what you want to include in your videos. Be confident, be excited, and be enthusiastic to share your knowledge.

Watch some TV and observe how exactly these folks, perform their trade, and borrow from them. Speak slightly faster than usual, and really talk to the people!

Your goal is to be fascinating, interesting, and somebody that's doing something great! Don't diss yourself, or play down your achievements.

As Donald Trump says: *"subtlety and modesty are appropriate for nuns, but if you're in business, you'd better learn to speak up and announce your significant accomplishments to the world."*

Roger Ailes wrote a fantastic book about this, which I strongly recommend, appropriately titled *You Are The Message*.

Dan Moskel

Chapter 6. Building Your Fan Club

Now, here we're looking to accomplish two goals: the first is to build a fence around your fans, and the second is to collect their contact information. This way we can continue to communicate with them, help them, sell your goods, and products. And continuously follow up with them, to nourish, and develop a beneficial relationship together.

Your Congregation

The unavoidable truth is the Justin Bieber fan club, are the most eager little ladies to hear his latest doings. While fever Bieber isn't my cup of tea, this principle applies to every business.

The most effective ways to build your congregation is with YouTube videos, as we've discussed. This includes your subscribers, because you can continue to communicate with them. And it extends to using a website, to collect your fans information. This enables your fans to raise their hand, and say yes, I want more of what you've got.

This list of fans, and followers is where the true gold lies, regardless if you're Stephen King, or Justin Bieber. It's the people that like you, and in business it's your customers that have found your goods, to be valuable, useful, and helpful.

Thus they're happy to have a relationship with you, and your business. After all Stephen King's fans are the most likely to buy his latest books, pay to hear him speak, and value his contribution to the world.

The Mechanics

The best way to collect your fans, contact information, so you can mimic the Bieber fever, and create a stampede of folks running off to buy your goods, is to use a website with a lead form. If you already have a website, this isn't new, and if you don't have one, we'll talk about the two ways to build this in the next chapter, without paying a fortune, or learning advanced calculous, just hang with me for a moment.

The goal here is to have a form that enables your fans to raise their hand. You should give them something of value to encourage them to do this. This can be the value added bonuses, we discussed earlier, or it can be some type of free report. It can truly be anything you want, but the more value your prospect and leads, see in this bribe the more likely they'll be to sign up and get it.

Technology empowers you to do this, very easily, and affordably. It also enables you to automate, as mush as you desire. For instance someone could sign up for your report, and then automatically it, along with email messages for the next five years, if you so choose.

This list of people is the equity in your business, and every business. For it's easier to sell goods to someone that knows you, and you can follow up with, than a stranger. It's smart to collect additional information. For example, you could offer to mail your lead, a free DVD in exchange for their physical mailing address.

The point is we need to collect a list, fan club, and people that like you, respect you, and want more of your expertise. If you've already got a list, you're ahead of the game, and have equity to work with. Great job, and keep it up.

Campaigns

You'll need to schedule a campaign and sequence of emails to be sent to your list. Obviously you can send any information you want, and a good message to send is your new compelling book description, to help drive some additional sales.

Naturally it's also good to send your fans, a message when you make new YouTube videos, publish a new article for your website, provide a live training event, the sky is the limit. As with all communications, it's key to view your message from the eyes of the receiver.

Get their attention with a good subject line, this is the headline, and you may want to use some of the popular keywords we've discussed. Because these fans, may have recently searched for that keyword, and if you're talking about it, you'll get their attention.

And don't neglect to ask, in your message! Ask your fans to go view your YouTube video, to read your new article, to buy your book, to do whatever it is you're asking of them. We must ask for everything we want in life, from what you're having for dinner, to your choice of careers, everything. Please, ask clearly, loudly, and specifically.

You'll need to use a list management service, or email marketing company to collect, and store your list of leads, send your messages, and provide you with a lead form. This can be done very inexpensively, and MailChimp currently provides you a way to get started for free. Obviously your account will have a few limitations, and we use Aweber, and Infusionsoft is a good one as well.

There's many services to choose from. When you add a lead form, all you do is copy and paste. It's easier than uploading a YouTube video, and using Facebook.

Testing

It's key to always test your messages, and any other media channels, you may be using. This is because the right answer is in the results. For the numbers don't lie.

It's much akin to being a scientist conducting experiments. The dollars are the answers, for our experiments. Test different messages, different subject lines, calls to action, test everything!

Technology today will show you exactly how your list responded and reacted. If they opened your message, clicked on the link in your call to action, and much more. This information is good to use with your further communications, and it's a key to email marketing, and any direct mail.

If you'd like to know more about email marketing, you can grab a copy of our book, <u>Email Marketing That Works ... So You Don't Have To</u>. We've learned a lot and used this lead generation tool, in our national TV commercial. Our call to action, was to visit our website, and sign up for our list.

It's important to always segment, segment, and segment. In other words, there's always ways to split up your fans into smaller groups. This way you can make your messages, more personalized, and customized to their specific, needs, wants, and interests.

Dan Moskel

Chapter 7. Articles

Now, that you're a professional writer, and have written a book, one of the ways in which you can build your fan base, is to write articles. You may want to submit these for publication to platforms that have an existing audience, such as: newspapers, magazines, websites, etc.

For example if you've written a book about investing, you'll likely be able to generate some interest by writing an article for Investors Business Daily. Please do make sure to plug, and mention your book, in any articles you write.

Create a Website

If you've already got a website, terrific. And if not, you can very easily and affordably create a website, and without learning advanced computer code. There's two ways to build a website. You can use WordPress and purchase web hosting, this is about $100 per year. And it will require you to learn some advanced computer geek language, and chances are outsource a few custom design jobs.

The other viable option is to build a website, using Blogger, a company owned by Google. And then place your site on a custom domain name, or URL address. This only costs about $15 a year. And if you can use Microsoft Word, or WordPerfect, you'll feel right at home with this technology.

For the full step by step details to use Blogger and build a new website, you can grab a copy of our book, _How To Create a Website - Easy Button_.

Visitors

You now, know a little bit about search engine optimization, and getting your website to show up at the top of the big three search engines. It's very wise to write articles about topics and subjects that have high search volume.

In other words, look at the Google Keyword Planner and write articles about the keyword terms that have a high number of searches.

This will target those terms, and increase your webpage's likelihood of showing up for those keyword searches.

And if you've already created videos, about these same topics. Please make sure that in your video description you include a link to your website, or a specific webpage on your site. For example, if you've made a video about the best chocolate chip cookie recipes, and you've got a page on your website about the same thing, make sure that your video, is voting for your website. And you're linking from the video, to your webpage.

Naturally, this also works the other way too. Instead, you could choose to link from your webpage, to your video.

I strongly encourage you to do this, by choosing anchor text, which is the words on a webpage that get hyperlinked. And this causes them to change colors, and it makes the words clickable. These words and anchor text should be the high volume keyword terms.

For instance, if you've got a page about chocolate chip cookie recipes, and a video about that keyword term, use the anchor text "*chocolate chip cookie recipes*" to link to your video. They're maybe some debate about this, but I prefer to create one way links.

In other words, if you link to your video from a webpage, then make sure inside that video, you aren't linking back directly to that same webpage. Instead link to a different page on your site. In other words, you don't want to cast a vote for one of your properties, and have that same property voting for your other property, that initially cast the first vote.

The idea is to have more votes, all going to one piece of property, rather than having your properties trade votes with one another.

Vote For Your Book

Now at the bottom of the articles on your website, please cast a vote over to your book at the online retailers. Here's the big picture idea with this funnel.

People search for a keyword in the search engines, and then they land on your website. Read your article, and at the bottom when you tell them if they want to know more, they can grab a copy of your book at Amazon. And you include a link over to your book at the online retailers. This makes it very easy for your website visitor, and article reader to click over and buy your book.

It also increases the popularity of your book. And finally it provides you with more sales, and royalties, our number one goal!

By the way, a great email marketing message to send to your list of fans, is that you've published a new article at your website. This'll help drive some initial visitors to check out your article.

Please, do let your list know if you publish an article at some bigger platforms, such as Investors Business Daily. This is instrumental in building your credibility, expertise, and even celebrity with your fans.

Dan Moskel

Chapter 8. Social Media

Naturally this includes Facebook, Google +, Twitter, Pinterest, and many more platforms. There's two objectives with using social media to market your book. The first of which is to drive sales, and the second is to build links. And thus increase your book's popularity at the online retailers.

It's wise to make a post with your new compelling book description, and share that on your social media profiles. Do include a link over to your book at the online retailers. This will make it easy for your friends, family, and colleagues to click over, and buy your book. Obviously, your casting a few more votes for your book at the online retailers, by doing this as well.

Please, don't invest a lot of time with social media. It's simply another avenue of communication. And trust me even the big box stores, you know the names, are hiring consultants to try and figure out how to earn money with social media.

The plain truth is royalties and your bank account, have no direct connection to the number of Facebook likes, Twitter followers, or Google + fans you have. Social media is the shiniest button of all with online marketing.

Stories abound like the woman on Shark Tank selling baby shoes, who discovered that 10% of her Instagram followers became customers. We also hear stories about people winning the lottery, that doesn't mean we should running off to invest with a credit card, in lottery tickets!

If you insist on investing big time here, please, make sure you're tracking so you know that your time, is producing dividends. And dividends that can be deposited at the bank! Not likes.

Too often we hear from entrepreneurs, who spend thousands of dollars on some whiz bang, fancy talking, internet marketing consultant, who promises them the moon with social media. And these business owners, are disappointed when they learn the expensive way, that just because people like you, that don't mean they're buying from you!

It's an amazing example of financial pornography. And believe me, these are smart people from doctors, lawyers, bakers, butchers, to candle stick makers.

With that said, there's two additional ways to use social media. When you make a new YouTube video, or publish a new article on your website, do share this with your Twitter followers, Facebook friends, and Google + fans.

This is going to build links to your article and website, along with your YouTube video. And those links, as we've discussed are votes. These votes will help your video, and article rank for when people search at YouTube and the search engines for keyword terms.

To clarify, when you make a YouTube video, or publish an article at your website, by sharing these on your social media profiles, with a link, your voting for those properties. This will make your properties, more popular.

It'll also help drive visitors to your articles, and viewers for your videos. And if you're plugging your book in your articles and videos, then it's an additional opportunity to sell more copies of your book.

Do you see how all this is connected? It's connected the same way that brick and mortar businesses are connected with everything they do. For you'd have to say a restaurant even with the best food, is doing a bad job selling you to return, if the bathroom is dirty

Chapter 9. Play With The Other Kids

There's three keys we're discussing here. The first is to use other people, such as, the established leaders in your niche, and their list of customers.

The second is to sell other good products, and services to your congregation of fans. And the third purpose is to provide maximum service to your followers, and thus earn maximum income.

Now, in your niche market there's already some established leaders with customers and fans. Did you know you can get these folks to sell your book to their followers?

Yup, it's true and it happens everyday. I'm sure you've received an email at some time, with a message promoting another company, person, or services.

In the industry it's called affiliate marketing. Some may prefer (JV) or joint venture, but the idea is simple.

You work with others, and they'll sell your book, products, and services. And this applies far beyond just selling books. In fact this is how our firm has earned millions of dollars starting in April, 2006, by selling other companies products and services for them! More on that, and how you can use this too, momentarily.

You're probably first wondering how to get other people to sell your book, for you? Ask! Ask! And ask again! Seriously, you have to ask other people!

And here's a secret, share the wealth! Let's be clear, other people will be happy to sell your book to their followers. Providing it's a good book, and you ask them to do this, along with paying them to. And we ain't talking about hourly wages, or providing medical insurance.

You see affiliate marketing is a pay per performance model, exactly like a commission based sales position. You'll only pay these guys, when they make a sale.

For instance, if they send an email to their list and sell 30 copies of your book. Then you'd pay them x amount for each one of those 30 sales. No more, no less, and no health care, or payroll tax!

You can also use a pay per lead model, so for every time someone fills out a form, you'd pay. Keep in mind you can also get paid this way.

You'll have to find a method to track your salesman's performance. There's a multitude of services for this including infusionsoft, and even the Amazon Associates program. That's the Amazon affiliate program, they just call it associates.

For some reason affiliate just doesn't sound nice, despite it's existence long before the advent of the internet. In fact, many Fortune 500 companies offer an affiliate program including iTunes, Amazon, American Express, and countless more.

Practically, every business doing anything online offers this. It's merely a sales position. That's it. We pay a commission and you'll see, how you can earn commissions too.

Maximum ROI

Now it may be a dirty little secret, but an effective way to earn maximum ROI, return on investment, for every business is to provide maximum value to your customers. And you can legally get paid more gold, for doing this.

Here's how it works, let's say you've got a list of 1,000 people, and they're interested in knowing more about chocolate chip cookie recipes. Now it only makes sense, that they'd also be interested in knowing what pan produces the best results, what type of chocolate chips to use, and what oven makes the best cookies.

The key here is you're the expert, you should tell them this information. Share with them what you use, what brand of chocolate chips is the best, and any other relevant information. The idea is to help them, and by helping them, and sharing more of yourself, you can earn more, if you utilize affiliate marketing.

Let's look at one more example, Perry Marshall, a big name in the copywriting, and direct response advertising industry. When our firm started out in business, in 2006, we we're only using pay per click advertising, with the big three search engines.

If you're unfamiliar, this is where you advertise in the sponsored results when someone searches for a keyword at Google. And you pay every time your ad is clicked upon and viewed. We we're targeting super competitive terms, paying up to two to three dollars per click!

We've spent HUGE piles of gold, and so much so, that Google even invited our firm out to tour their campus. You see, the only reason we were able to use this and profitably, to earn millions of dollars, selling other companies goods and services. Is because of a lot of diligent work, and deploying direct response advertising fundamentals in our marketing.

This empowers you and our firm, to methodically pursue profitable traffic avenues, and cut the fat on wasteful spending. It holds your advertising accountable. And thus, enables everyone who uses it to earn great, big, piles of cold hard cash!

This is the only intelligent way to advertise, operate, and run a business. By measuring what's producing gold, for the numbers don't lie. This is precisely how the late great Billy Mays produced his fortune, and countless others.

Now Perry Marshall wrote a book, *The Definitive Guide To Google AdWords*, that's the name of the Google online advertising platform (AdWords). This information was priceless to me, and without a doubt has contributed significantly to my lifetime earnings!

Many years after reading it, I meet Perry while working at a Ken McCarthy Systems Seminar event, in Chicago. And have become good friends with him. Certainly you'd agree that I'd be derelict to not share with my friends, family, coworkers, and my list how much Perry's information has helped and benefited me.

And after a lot of my persistent badgering, Perry finally relented, and has created a sweet deal for his newest book *80/20 Sales and Marketing*. For folks that are on my list, Perry will let me send them an email, with a link over to this book at his website where they can get it for just one penny. Rather than the current Amazon price of $15.63.

The Book Marketing Plan

Here's the cool part, Perry will payout $7.00 for every person that does get his book for a penny. That means using our earlier example, if you sent an email to your list, promoting Perry's offer and generated 30 sales, you'd earn $210 for that one email.

What's that work out to, a few minutes of your time invested, and a $210 return on your investment. That sounds good to me. And further by only recommending good, valuable, useful information you're helping your list of fans, and followers.

The reason Perry can pay $7.00 when he's only charging one penny, is because he know's his numbers. This isn't the only structure, often you can pay other people just a percentage of the sale price, or split the revenue with them.

But Perry's a savvy businessman, and he knows a reader of his book is worth more than $7.00. Many businesses operate this way, paying out money on an initial sale, or even for a lead, and prospect. Because they know they'll earn more gold on the back end.

These are often businesses that are good at creating a relationship with their customers, and clients. And a mutually beneficial relationship at that.

I've been telling people for years about how great Perry is. He's one of a few good marketers, with sound proven advice. You can see, I'd be doing this regardless if Perry offered an affiliate program or not. And will continue to because it's that helpful. And I encourage you to investigate Perry if you're a serious marketing student.

The Best Value

Can you see how recommending books, products, goods, and services that you've found useful is helping your fans, and followers? Along with providing them more value?

Obviously and we do this in normal life with our family, and friends all the time. A few last examples include web hosting for a website, we use BlueHost, or an email marketing service such as AWeber, we use this as well. Heck, even suggesting people read *The Count of Monte Cristo* by Alexandre Dumas.

You can use the Amazon Associates program. And there's countless other affiliate networks, and you'll be able to work with some companies directly. The unavoidable truth is the people want you to share what you've found useful, just like your family and friends.

So you should do this, and it's not like you're doing anything you don't do already. And give the people what they want, and that is you, my friend! If you'd like to know more about this revenue model, you can grab a copy of our book _The Blueprint To Affiliate Marketing_. For every success book preaches selling is the most valuable skill. And when you can do it effectively, companies will line up at your door, with big bags of gold asking for your help.

Dan Moskel

Chapter 10. Advertising

Listen, advertising your book can launch your career as an entrepreneur. We'll discuss a few examples, and strategies, momentarily. First, the key concept to grasp, is your book is just another form of media.

It should attract clients, fans, followers, and these are the best quality leads. Because you've already had an opportunity to demonstrate your value, expertise, and created a relationship with them. Just think about it.

What a book does is attract customers that've already purchased from you, trust you, and value your expertise. You're the guy. And these people value your opinion, a whole lot more than a casual TV viewer, or a random person off the street, or even a stranger walking into your shop. They know you!

Robert Ringer began his career as a self published author. And using offline advertising he catapulted multiple books to the New York Times best seller list. He then leveraged this into multiple revenue streams by offering consulting, speaking, information products, coaching, and publishing more books.

Certainly, you've seen the snake oil salesman, Kevin Trodeau, and his TV infomercials. Hawking books about everything under the sun, before he went to jail. Well, my friend, people were standing in line to throw money at him, and he had at least a half a screw loose.

And if you were born before 1980, you're sure to remember the question mark guy, Matthew Lesko. This gentleman ran TV infomercials for years selling his books, about how to get free money from the government. By happenstance, we ran into Matthew a few years back in New York City, a very nice man, and yes, he was decked out in his riddler looking suit.

You may be surprised to learn that he initially sold his services to Fortune 500 companies, and later shifted to helping, average, everyday people. The ones that would benefit the most with his information.

The big picture here is to be creative, and see how you can make the media work for your book, and more importantly for your business. Let me share this last non book marketing example, before we get into the nuts and bolts.

Jay Abraham a direct response marketing legend, who Damon John of The Shark Tank says is a mentor to him. Has an incredible story of building the ICY HOT brand.

You see, this little fledgeling company was purchased, and with no substantial advertising budget. In short order, they were marketing through a variety of media channels, and for free.

You see, for every ten new ICY HOT customers, eight of them would reorder the next month, and this would continue forever. Thus, Jay worked out deals with a number of partners where the media outlet, a radio station for example, would get paid on performance.

They'd get paid 100% of the initial sale price, for all the sales that a specific media channel generated. In fact, they were able to pay more than a 100%, because they knew their numbers. And were certain they'd earn a multiple of that with the *Customers Lifetime Value* or CLV.

The point with all this is don't write off advertising, because you can't see how selling a book, could produce any more income than the measly $2 royalty you earn. In the world of good business, we want to make as many media channels work for an offer, as possible, and profitably.

Direct Response

As we've mentioned using direct response principles is the only wise way of advertising, for every business. You must ask people to do exactly what it is you want, and measure your results.

There's two things to note, the first is this approach to advertising is scientific. It empowers you to determine precisely how must each lead, and or sale is costing you. And you can also see the CLV, or *Customer Lifetime Value*.

You see, if you know for certain that spending $500 on an ad, will generate 50 leads, with a value of $1,500 in profits. You can go out and buy boatloads of media!

It's unfortunate because if you ask most business owners what their advertising is producing. You'll hear them stutter, mumble, and fart around, until they finally confess they haven't a clue. That's NO WAY to run a business!

The second item of note, is we must continuously test, and test everything including your follow up campaign. Everything we do, can always be better. Once you've discovered a control ad and a profitable funnel, buying more media is the easy part.

These principles apply to selling your book, and every product, and service. That's simply the deliverable, the goods. It's interchangeable, but the system of selling and marketing with direct response is the special sauce, and has universal application.

This gives you certainty. And that's a whole lot better than, hoping, wishing, and praying your advertising dollars are bringing people in the door, and making sales. Hoping, wishing, and praying in business is blasphemy!

It's like playing the lottery with a credit card investment. You'd better hope, pray, and wish, you hit the jackpot! And listen to my testimony, most people that preach about branding, couldn't sell their way out of a paper bag! Let's be wise and follow the dollars!

Offline Media

This is the traditional old school media including: newspapers, magazines, direct mail, radio, TV commercials, and more. The big takeaway is the "rate cards" or initial price quotes should be filed under fiction.

You can always negotiate with media channels for more reasonable rates. It's important to test as inexpensively as possible, and obviously measure.

If you've got some data, and systems in place, you could pursue the ICY HOT path and get creative. By the way that's just one business, that was built using media with a pay per performance structure. But, this sure ain't the only business that's been built with this model.

The best approach is to view all media channels, as though they've got to prove their value. As in they've got a responsive audience.

In other words, the pressure's on them to provide you with the audience, customers, and leads, you want to advertise to. And people that'll buy your goods.

The pressure isn't on you to buy their services. You're one of the few, wise, savvy entrepreneurs that views advertising dollars in the same light, as investing dollars. The only time we part with them, is so they can go out and bring us back more dollars. We ain't branding here, we're selling, and mining for gold!

Take note when you're negotiating with these media channels, if you commit to a longer term media buy, they'll be eager to work with you on lower prices. But do make sure to test first, before you make a long term commitment.

Naturally, it's easier to do this once you've created a control, that you know works. The objective I want you to be aware of, is that you're in the drivers seat. If only because you've got the gold that these media channels want in advertising revenue.

Online Media

Online media is a god send. It empowers advertisers to set a pin point laser target, on their perfect ideal customers.

First, this includes pay per click with the big three search engines. This way you can advertise to people searching for specific keyword terms. You can also target your audience based upon their location, and much more demographic information.

There's also the content or display network, which is buying advertising space on another website, such as a banner ad. And of course YouTube advertising, Facebook, and many more avenues.

Online media is great not only because it works, but you can accurately target an audience. And avoid the expense of advertising to people that are not your ideal customers. It's very easy, and inexpensive to test. And with technology we can automate, and create some very effective multi-media sales funnels.

For example as we've shared, it's all about the relationship you have with your fans. So let's say they've searched for the keyword "*entrepreneur*" at Google. You could have an ad in the sponsored results. And when they click on it they'd hit a landing page, or squeeze page, where you're offering them a free widget, in exchange for their email address.

Once they comply with your first request, you could then funnel them to the next page, where you're offering to mail them a companion DVD to their house. Doing this, will enable you to first segment your list, from serious leads, those that want a companion DVD. And less interested prospects, who only provide their email address.

And if you're still living in the stone age, direct mail works! Collecting a leads, physical address will enable you to send follow up marketing pieces. And continue to build your relationship both online and offline.

You see, our goal is to build systems that attract not just sales and book royalties, but the best people, fans, and customers to do additional businesses with us. Be that buying more books, coaching, consulting, the sky's the limit.

The Pareto principle pioneered in 1906, by the Italian economist Vilfredo Pareto, also know as the 80/20 rule. Says that for businesses they'll earns 80% of their profits, from just 20% of their customers. And it's true!

Our objective is to engineer the ideal, perfect business for you. By making you attractive to the best customers in your market, because you're running the best business, providing the best value. And this is measured in dollars, and thus you'll be earning the best profits.

By the way, if you happen to advertise with both online and offline media, and with the same outlet, you may be able to leverage this when negotiating advertising prices. For example, if you're perfect customer, client, or patient is a reader of Entrepreneur magazine. And you buy advertising space in the magazine, and also want space on their website. This should get you a reduction in price. Obviously it's more volume and revenue for them.

Chapter 11. Be Omnipresent

Many moons ago, an early business mentor said to thee, you want to be everywhere. The loneliest number in business is one. Only one way to sell, one way to distribute your goods, one type of media to advertise with, and only one way to earn gold.

This has two applications, the first is specific to your distribution channels because you can publish your book at a number of leading online retailers. This'll help produce more sales and royalties for you, and below we've listed the top six distribution avenues.

Naturally there are additional avenues, and if you discover some profitable streams of gold elsewhere, please let us know, so we can share it with the others. And of course, we'll be happy to give you full credit, and a plug for your book.

1. Amazon

Obviously, Amazon is the big swinger in the online book retail industry. If you're self publishing and use CreateSpace.com, a company owned by Amazon, you'll automatically have your book listed at Amazon. Along with being able to choose expanded distribution. If you choose this option your book will also be available at BarnesandNoble.com, along with libraries, academic institutions, and additional online retailers.

2. Kindle

Of course, it's wise to publish your book on the Kindle as many people consume books electronically, these days. So follow the money! You can and should include links in your electronic books, so as to make it easy for people to act on your call to action, inside your book.

   For example if you're asking your reader to visit your website and sign up for their free bonus gift, then include a link to your website, so they can just click over and comply with your request.

3. iTunes

Yes, you can publish your book electronically at iTunes. You'll need an iTunes Connect account and they'll sell your book for you, and pay you gold in royalties.

4. Google Play

Google Play is one of the newest online book retail platforms, with significant distribution that all authors should take advantage of. It strikes me as a bit odd, being an old school paper and pen guy, but people buy electronic books and they but a lot of them. We as entrepreneurs must adapt to the market, so we can earn maximum gold.

5. Barnes and Noble Nook

The Nook is the Barnes and Noble electronic device, just like Amazon's Kindle. Obviously, this platform doesn't have as large a distribution as the Kindle, but it's still an effective place to publish your book. And you'll see returns, because they do sell books here, as well.

6. Audio Book

If you've yet to discover the new Amazon platform, audible.com, now is the time. This is publishing your book in spoken word audio format, so your reader can listen, rather than read.

This is a prime place to publish your book. Amazon is doing a lot of advertising, and marketing to bring new users to the audible.com platform. And I personally predict and have seen a shift in consumption, in favor of audio. Of course, this has existed long before the internet, but it's an effective location to earn gold, right now.

You can use acx.com to upload your audio files, and from here you can also find professional voice over talent, if you prefer someone else does the narration. Naturally you can also do this yourself.

Should you choose to hire a professional narrator and use acx.com, then you'll have two methods to pay them. You can split the royalties or you can pay on a per completed hour basis.

If you've got a proven winner and your book is selling in the print version, then it'd be wise, and most cost effective to pay per hour. But if you're hoping to escape going to work at The Office with Michael Scott, and Dwight Schrute, it's wise to focus on time effectiveness, and prioritize earning more gold.

Now once you've published your audio book, the listing page and description of your book at Amazon, will change. Your book at Amazon, will now have a listen button.

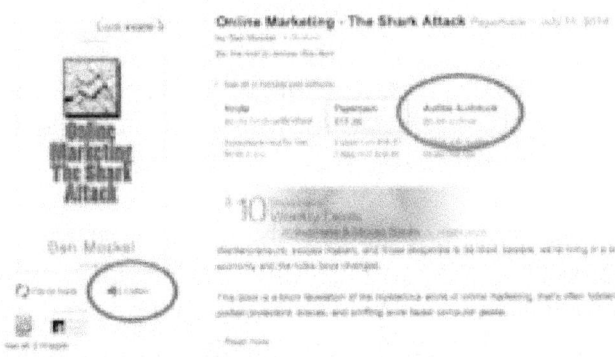

My suspicion is this helps your book at Amazon, if only because it'll make you appear as a more professional author. You've published your book in print, electronic format, and in audio. And I'd suspect that potential readers, will make a similar assumption about the books that are available in all these formats, rather than merely electronically.

Obviously it's more engaging to hear someone's voice, than read their words. So this listen button may be responsible for additional book sales, even in the print version and electronic format. On an aside, you'll be able to choose a retail sample of your book in audio.

This should be your compelling book description, because potential readers of your book, will naturally judge and make their decision based upon this material. You do have a small written section for the audio platform, as well. And acx.com will automatically make your book available for purchase in audio at Audible, Amazon, and iTunes.

The big benefit to publishing on all these platforms, beyond creating additional streams of royalties and gold deposits hitting your bank account. Is when you can tell your audience in your marketing materials (videos, articles, emails) that your book is available at Amazon, iTunes, Google Play, Barnes and Noble, audio book, and in the Kindle, and Nook, it sounds much more professional.

This helps to give you more credibility, expertise, and authority. Than merely saying your book is available on the Kindle, at Amazon. It's key to find ways to increase your trust, credibility, and positioning yourself as the expert with your audience.

Dan Moskel

Chapter 12. Automatic Sales Funnels

Here's the deal, our automatic sales funnels that we'll review in a moment, is the second application of being omnipresent.

You see, if people are looking for information about your specific topic in YouTube, the search engines, and the online retailers. We want them to always find you!

We want you to be inescapable, and for it be impossible for interested folks, not to find your material! We want YOU to be everywhere!

Keep in mind, just as there's persuasive writing, the same system applies to media. And in marketing this is called copywriting.

You must first get their attention, and offer help, value, and service. And then you should persuade your audience, to do what it is you want. Be it buying your book, visiting your website and signing up for a free report, or simply subscribing to your YouTube channel.

And ask for what it is you want, clearly, loudly, and specifically. For Jesus said in the Sermon on The Mount:

"Enter by the narrow gate; for wide is the gate and broad is the way that leads to destruction, and there are many who go in by it. Because narrow is the gate and difficult is the way which leads to life, and there are few who find it."

Yes, setting up these six automatic sales funnels isn't easy, nor should it be. Once you set up a few, you should always build more, so you can earn more!

The two big keys for every message include having fun, being energetic, interesting, and even fascinating. The second is to be of service, first, then ask for what it is you want. Along with providing reasons and benefits for your audience to comply with your request.

Don't lose sight of the fact that you will get better, with everything, the more you do it. It seems that when we become adults, we forget this basic life lesson. And try to be perfect, and flawless, rather than always trying to get better.

One of the principles we preach is it's not ABC, or always be closing, but ABL, always be learning. The plain truth is you can never know too much about who your serving, and selling something too. And what their specific motivations are, and precisely why they'll buy.

To tie all this together, we're going to review the six automatic sales funnels and how exactly they'll make you omnipresent in your niche.

1. YouTube Videos

Once you have videos ranking for keyword searches at YouTube, then you'll be getting automatic views on your videos. These views will be people looking for information about your topic. And thus highly qualified, and interested prospects, the most likely folks to buy your book. Surely more than a random guy on the street.

Currently, between our three YouTube channels, we get about 600 daily views. Yes, about 600 people, every single day, hear that our books exist.

Now, don't you see how you'll sell a handful of your books, here and there. When there's always more, and new people discovering you, every single day! Of course and I've got the gold deposits to prove it!

2. Articles

If you've been using the information contained within these pages. Then you'll be able to get some natural, organic, search engine traffic to your website. Just by using good keyword rich titles for your articles, and building links to become popular.

This'll empower your website to be discovered by people searching for your information, at Google, Yahoo, and Bing. And then when these folks read your articles, you'll have a call to action with a link at the end of your article. Asking them to go and purchase your book, and a handful of people will do this.

3. Email Marketing

As you discover some good messages that convert, with your email marketing campaigns. This should be messages selling your own books, products and services.

But also messages with complimentary goods, and services. So you can maximize your earnings, and the service you provide.

Once you find these, you can set up campaigns that'll run automatically, for as long as you desire. As an example, you could create a funnel that when someone signs up and joins your congregation, they'll automatically get 10 messages over the next 15 days. And you don't have to do a lift a finger, except to sign and deposit the checks.

Of course you should do a whole lot more. And provide as much engagement, and excitement, as you can to build the best relationship with your fans.

In other words, give the people what they want and that my friend is YOU. Share with them your expertise, your books, your knowledge, and yourself!

4. Advertising

If you pursue this path, you can easily set up your advertisements to run for weeks, months, even years. So long as it continues to be profitable.

There's a little bit of maintenance, and a lot initially to weed out the waste, and cut the fat. Once you've worked out the tweaks, you really just have to write the checks after that.

In other words, the time investment once you build a winning funnel, is very minimal maintenance. And it'll produce new customers, and clients, as reliably as a great grandfather clock ticks.

5. Partners

As you cultivate and nourish some good relationships with the leaders in your niche, and related categories. You'll be able to have them go out and sell your books for you. Again, this is another automatic sales funnel, because you're only lifting a finger, to sign the checks.

6. Online Retailer Searches

Now, if you're creating videos, publishing articles, and linking to your book at the online retailers. You're building your book's popularity.

This'll help you increase your rankings and show up when people search for keywords at Amazon, for example. Now if your new compelling book description page, is being viewed a whole lot more, by people looking for a book about your topic. Don't you think a handful of people here and there will be buying your book?

The answer is YES! And there's abundant evidence, and gold to back this up.

Moving To Higher Ground

The unavoidable truth is this wont happen overnight. Please, do use all six of these funnels and follow the money!

Some of these automatic sales funnels will be more profitable, and faster. They all work, effectively, and many are evergreen and will last a lifetime.

As you see returns, use it as jet fuel to keep building. The city made of gold, Dubai, is the best example. They've got a plethora of modern Wonders of our World, and they're continuing to build more.

Last I heard they're building a city, indoors. This continuous pursuit is what makes you, and the city of Dubai, the best! Marketing your book is the most important aspect of writing a book and being successful with it.

Keep in mind, the more you do, the more you earn! And I guarantee you it feels awesome to wake up in the morning, and see more sales, royalties, and gold you've earned while you were sleeping!

Please, don't neglect your fan club, because all these media avenues are simply tools to communicate. Our focus is on building a relationship. And thus you need to communicate and send messages, frequently. In order to sell your goods, and also to provide maximum value.

Let your fans know when you publish a new article, video, have events, anything exciting, and noteworthy. These are the people that are most interested in receiving that information.

And for the first 100 people that join our congregation at DanMoskelUniversity.com, we're offering you a free review of your book description page. For the cold harsh truth is the market doesn't give a flip about what you want, and it doesn't matter how many people see your book exists, if your message doesn't convert viewers into buyers. The only way to sell more books, products, and services, is to create a message the market will respond to!

Dan Moskel

Chapter 13. KDP Select Promotions

Look, we could devote massive time to many book retailer deal sites, or one off promotional tools. But this leaves you always looking for new customers, much like a drug addict looking for his next fix. You see, we need to do both. Build automatic sales funnels that will last a lifetime, and mine gold from our existing fans.

With that said, the most powerful promotional tools is the Amazon KDP Select. This is a free feature, that you can enroll in when you publish your book, on the Kindle. There's been a number of updates over the years, and these continue so please visit their website for full terms and conditions.

How It Works

You'll be given access to two promotional tools for a five day period, inside a 90 day window. The catch is you must give the electronic version of your book, exclusively to the Kindle, in order to use these promotion weapons.

In other words, you can NOT have your book available electronically at iTunes, on the Barnes and Noble Nook, Goggle Play or anywhere else. You can still sell the print and audio versions, just not the electronic version at other retailers.

You can opt out, and opt in for these features, so long as you follow the guidelines. I'd be wise to test and experiment, and see what the results provide you.

Free Promotion

The first promotional weapon is running a free giveaway. Naturally you'll be able to put your book in a number of people's hands. Our best giveaway was about 500 copies of a book. This tool also helps to make your book more discoverable at Amazon.

The big problem with this method is your giving it away for free. This isn't a problem from the perspective of earning royalties. You see, giving anything away, especially when it comes to information, is much like giving away advice.

It's in abundance! And people don't value it, if only because it is free. If for no other reason, than it's free, most people won't bother to read it. I'd encourage you to instead use this second promotion weapon, which is a countdown deal.

Countdown Deal

This alternative feature enables you to offer for a limited time, a discounted price. For instance, you could offer your book for sale for $1.99, instead of the regular $7.99 price.

Amazon will help put your book with it's discounted price, in front of more people. And you can domino this by sending an email message to your existing list of fans, letting them know about your deal. And sharing it with your followers on social media.

One of the coolest features of the countdown deal, is that you'll be able to set different price increments, across the five days you run a discount. This can give you data into the sweet spot price point, inside your niche. And I suggest you test to find the best price point for your book.

Obviously a limited time, price discount, will help to add urgency to your compelling book description. And convert more people that view your book, into buyers! I do suggest you investigate and at least experiment with these promotional features, with Amazon.

Pricing

Now I've got a lot to say about pricing your goods, but not much about your book. Currently when you publish on the Kindle, you'll get access to see what the best price point is. This is a new feature and the only way to truly discover, is to test, and run experiments.

The key fundamental and there's been a lot of research on this, we human beings place more value on things we pay more money for. Naturally. A new $300 pair of jeans is more valuable than your old, beat up Levi's. We value a luxury car, more than a KIA.

Most businesses underprice, and under value their service. And you'd be shocked to hear some of the stories of clients we work with. And just how much more they've earned, just by raising their prices.

Reviews

Listen, my friend, most book reviews are worthless. You see, many online reviews are manufactured. Bob Bly, the author of over 70 books, said it best when he shared the story of getting a negative review, because the woman didn't like the paper his book was printed on.

The cold harsh truth is that most people are bitter, angry, and mad at the world! And they'll be quick as a jack rabbit to let you and anyone know about it.

Look, no further than Monday morning quarterbacks, that'll criticize a team even when they win! Dude, you're sitting in the lay-z-boy, recliner, drinking a duff beer. Respectfully you don't know diddly! It's akin to gathering up ye fellow flanderinos and complaining to them how Mr. Burns just needs to pay his fair share in taxes.

Authors often get discouraged by these "haters" as Oprah calls them. And believe me, my friend, they're in abundance! They're the last people anyone should ever listen to! And often the least qualified to be giving advice, feedback, or leaving a review.

These folks are the spectators in life, and really don't matter. For the people that do matter, will be happy you're at least doing something. Rather than hoping, and wishing to suck the metaphorical tit of the government, and Mr. Burns tax dollars.

One method of getting reviews for your book, is to outright ask your readers inside your book to leave a review. And I'll ask you right now, to leave a positive review if you've enjoyed this book.

Reviews do provide social proof to potential buyers of your book, but it's really not where you should invest your time. There's much more profitable investments to make. Let me share with you a quote from Jeff Bezos, the founder of Amazon: "If you never want to be criticized, for goodness sake don't do anything new." And I'd even extend it to doing anything at all.

To further this just a bit, when we ran our national TV commercial appearing on ESPN, MTV, A&E, VH-1, Comedy Central, and many more. We used a call to action asking viewers to visit our website and sign up for a free report.

Now when we provided our website URL address or domain name, we said backslash TV. Instead of the appropriate term slash, stroke, or whatever you may prefer to call it.

Holy heavens! The response we received was incredible! These crazy people sent us unspeakable messages, and you'd have thought I was the anti-christ for saying backslash instead, of slash.

Yet, didn't even these "haters" get where I wanted them to go, my website? Yes, they did!

It was a mistake. And the point is the world is full of spectators, just waiting to jump all over anyone's mistakes. And that's one of the big keys to becoming successful, being aware that people won't like you, if for no other reason, than because they can see you.

Don't worry, these folks don't like much in this world! And they certainly can't play baseball better than Michael Jordan, or throw a football better than Tom Brady. They're the spectators! Reviews will happen, both good and bad, for every book.

Heck, there's people on YouTube that don't like the Sermon on the Mount. Come'on man! Step your game up! The point is don't stress the details, and keep in mind the people that mind, don't matter. And those that matter, don't mind. After all, I'm much happier seeing someone try to do something, than hearing them complain about Mr. Burns and Scrooge McDuck being the cause for their misfortune.

Chapter 14. Media Interviews

Now that you're a published author, you've already or will be receiving requests from media outlets, for interviews. This can be a great source of publicity and a shot of steroids for your book marketing efforts, if you use it wisely.

To clarify, you'd better do you homework, and find ways in which to plug and mention your book exists, so the audience can go buy it. This sounds obvious, but let's look at an example to see just how powerful this is.

Recently, I received an email and below we've included the meat of this message. Please, think how you would respond to getting a message such as this:

Dear Dan,

I hope this message finds you well. Kindly I would like to interview you for the Be Efficient TV show about your expertise, career and ventures. The interview will take about an hour, but it might take from 50-80 minutes based on the conversation flow.

If the above sounds good to you, we can set the interview 3 to 7 days from today. I always prefer any time to start the interview between 1 to 3 pm Dubai Time.

Be Efficient TV Mission
To Boost the efficiency of your life and business with tips and tricks from leading experts

Regards,
Ahmed Al Kiremli
Founder & Host
Be Efficient Tv
http://ahmedalkiremli.com

What Would You Do?

What would you do, how would you respond to this request? The plain truth is many folks make big assumptions, just on someone's name like Ahmed. Let me tell you what I did, first I replied I'd be happy to talk with him. And then I ran off and did my homework, to discover and learn who I'd be talking with.

Wouldn't you know it, Ahmed lives in the city of Gold, Dubai, a part of the United Arab Emirates. Which according to Forbes magazine, the United Arab Emirates is the 6th richest country in the world, just edging out the United States at number seven.

This means the audience for our interview has lots of gold. And if we've got value to provide, many folks will be happy to exchange their gold, for our goods. After all we do live in a global economy, and your book can be sold all over the world.

It gets even better my new friend, Ahmed, is a speaker who gave a Ted Talk in 2013. He was born in Iraq, and today he's risen up to become a very successful entrepreneur, running multiple businesses. One of which includes *Iraqi Touch*, a unique casual food experience. Currently accepting applications for franchisees.

And if you happen to visit the city of gold, Dubai, please do visit his restaurant, and tell him that Dan Moskel sent you. I've no doubt he'll welcome you with open arms!

You see, Ahmed is currently writing a book to help others go from an employee to an entrepreneur. And he discovered me thru my 8th book, _How To Write a Book - The System_.

Please, do check out Ahmed. He's an awesome guy with a spectacular story of success and you can hear a subsequent interview of him, on my Dan Moskel YouTube channel. Naturally, we felt compelled to reciprocate and interview Ahmed and share his uplifting, encouraging, and positive message with our fans. And will be one of the first people to buy his book, as soon as it's available.

The Moral

The moral of all this is that it's wise to do you homework, for every media interview. Rehearse and mentally prepare, and plan how the interview will go. This principle applies aptly to speaking as well. And the fact that everything you do is marketing.

It's mission critical to find ways to say what you want to say, and link it to your goods. For example, you could say how in your book, you talked extensively about that point.

You see, imply mentioning your goods exist, is marketing. This is a soft sell, rather than a hard sell where you ask your audience to go buy your book, right now.

Craft a unique message for all your audiences, all the time. Keep in mind, you can never know too much about who you're talking too, selling your book too, and communicating with.

I'm not suggesting you start conducting background checks on people, but do invest a moment putting the bigger picture pieces of the puzzle together. Starting with who exactly the audience is, who is interviewing you, and what's most applicable, relevant, and pertinent to them. And don't neglect to share your accomplishments with the world.

You want to be somebody and larger than life. This is one of the big secrets to attracting maximum wealth with your book.

Dan Moskel

Chapter 15. The Disney Lesson

Listen my friend, it's a plain truth that most breakthroughs in business require you to look outside of your particular industry. This is using funnel vision, and Disney is a perfect example.

Now one of the few drawbacks for guests visiting Disney World, was the wait in line to get on a ride. Admittedly this is a good problem, and far superior than not having enough guests visiting your establishment.

How did Disney go about turning this problem into a strength? They looked to the restaurant industry, and borrowed from them. Surely, you've been to a busy restaurant and were issued a beeper type device, that would light up, and flash when you're table is ready. Today, Disney World, now uses this same type of device, to let people know their done waiting in line, and can get on a ride. Brilliant!

The point with this story, is you must find ways to use these book marketing weapons. Don't write them off, because you can't see how they'll work. Make them work for you! Find a way!

It's amazing how people instinctively look for all the reasons why they can't do something, rather than all the ways they can! Be smart and be an adult about running your business. You've got a complex problem with how to earn more money from your book. That's what every author wants and it requires complex solutions.

You see, when I was a boy I interned at Disney World. And they create complex systems to operate their one of a kind business, all the way down to taking out the trash. And they don't try to make anything perfect.

Perfection is the ultimate shinny button in life. Nothing's perfect. Michael Jordan, never played a perfect basketball game, where he didn't miss a shot. But he played good enough to be the best in the world! Disney doesn't try to create perfect rides, they make great stuff and then find ways to plus it. How can we make it better?

The weapons we've discussed for marketing your book is all about adding pluses. It's about making your book more attractive to buy. Manufacturing a better experience, and creating a relationship with your customers. Rather than a one night stand, or outcome.

Marketing Inside Your Book

Now if you've been paying attention, you've noticed we've shared with you about a number of additional books I've written. If you haven't noticed it's because we used a soft sell, and casually mentioned it. Along with inviting you to visit DanMoskelUniversity.com and sign up for your free bonus gifts.

You see, by sharing with your reader that you have additional products, services, and goods, they know about them. Thus if they're interested, they can buy them. We by design want more from the people, we trust in life. The people we know, and businesses that provide excellent value. This is the relationship.

Look to Disney, they create and nourish a relationship with their fans, guests, and customers. Every movie they make, is marketing their amusement parks. Certainly, you also see how their Pirates of the Caribbean ride was marketing the movies?

Of course! It's wise to find ways to sell, and casually mention your additional products and services. Because when your readers trust you, and build a relationship with you, they'll want more of you and your valuable goods. This is how Oprah was able to domino her TV show into a television network, magazine, and an empire. It was the relationship she created with her viewers.

For every business is fundamentally a marketing business. This is how you bring people in the door, and convince them to exchange their gold, for your valuable book, products, goods, and services. Along with delivering. And I'd encourage you to over deliver. This will enable your customers to easily come back and continue to exchange their gold for your goods.

This is unlike Jim Carey's character Lloyd, in the first *Dumb and Dumber* movie. Where he sold a decapitated bird to the little blind boy,

Billy. Despite Lloyd's belief that he took care of this problem, using duct tape. It'll be virtually impossible for Lloyd to sell Billy any additional goods.

Dan Moskel

Chapter 16. Story Telling

Peter Guber author of *Tell To Win* a #1 New York Times bestseller, who is also the CEO and chairman of Mandalay Entertainment, along with being a co-owner of the Golden State Warriors, and L.A. Dodgers. And he's produced multiple box office hits including Rain Man, Batman, The Color Purple, and more.

In his majestic book, he shares the story of when he was a boy. And a kid in the neighborhood who was physically and mentally handicapped, use to watch him and the other kids ride their bike up and down the street.

This boy with the help of his dad, and a unique bike, was struggling one afternoon trying to ride his bike up and down the street, just like the other children. On one of these spectacular wipeouts, Peter ran over to help the boy up, but was stopped in his dead in his tracks. By his father knocking on the window and telling him not too.

Peter was so touched he went home and told his mom. He wanted to help the boy, and believed his dad wasn't treating him right. When a few moons later, he saw the boy riding up and down the street, and doing what he'd decided to do. And saw him and his dad laughing, crying, and shouting with joy for his achievement.

The moral that stuck with Peter throughout his life, was just how directly connected success and failure truly are. You can not succeed with anything in life without the willingness to fail, to fall, and to get back up.

You will make mistakes. Their will be adversity, their will be challenges. And anyone whose achieved enduring success, will be the first to tell you how connected success and failure are. You see, Michael Jordan, nor LeBron James can make the game winning shots, without taking on the risk of failure and missing. And believe me, they've missed, along with myself, and hopefully you too. Because the only way you can make a shot in life, is to risk missing, risk losing, risk failing and risk falling.

The Book Marketing Plan

As Zig Ziglar used to say, it's not about how far you fall, but rather how high you bounce back up. By the way, Zig was initially a self published author with many years of struggle, set back, and temporary defeat.

We as human beings are programmed for stories. We relate to stories. And story telling is a craft, a skill, and an ability we cultivate and become better at. It's a powerful device to use, with your book and all your marketing materials.

Look no further than Ayn Rand's best selling book *Atlas Shrugged*. This book has sold over seven million copies, and is ranked as the second most influential book, only to the Bible. If you're unfamiliar with Ayn Rand, she's an immigrant to America, from Communist Russia. Where as a young girl, she witnessed the criminal thugs, or politrickesters, come in and take her family's business away.

She weaved these experiences into her literature, and injected her philosophy into her fictional stories. Her influence and contribution to our world, continues to this day. And is what America was built upon. She predicted many of our financial crises in our brave new world. And she squarely placed the blame on the takers, also known as the politicians. And the false idea that you exist for someone else's well being.

Did you know Ayn Rand was ridiculed, criticized, and condemned by the so called expert reviewers? Yet her legacy and this book continue to positively influence millions of people.

Chapter 17. Maximum ROI

Look, publishing a book makes you attractive to wealth. It makes you much more attractive for other people to give you their gold for your knowledge, experience, and wisdom. However, there's an important key to learn from Kevin O'Leary of the hit TV show, The Shark Tank.

You see, my brother Kevin, schedules his day in 30 minute increments, and it's all based upon ROI, or return on investment. Now that you've written a book, and are creating videos and communicating with your fan club, you'll get a lot of mail!

Some of these folks will just want to pass along their gratitude, thanks, and if you're single like me, you may receive a few marriage proposals. Other folks will want you to help them, and some of these folks will feel entitled to your help.

They believe that you owe them your time, and you should give it to them for free. As if you're just waiting around on a Saturday morning, for their email, where they're flailing about and demanding that you help them, and give them your time. As Dan Kennedy calls these folks, they're the time vampires. They'll suck you dry, and complain about how you didn't wipe their backside with the soft toilet paper.

Now it's true, you must give before you can get. But one of the rarely discussed truths about successful people, is they have an endless number of folks all wanting their time, even for lucrative partnerships, and paid consulting.

But time vampires and unreasonable people, should be avoided like the black plague. This is your business and you should engineer it, to meet your needs, your wants, your desires, and not Bob's wishes. People are people, and the only difference between a client paying you $100 per hour, and $1,000 per hour, is the amount of money you earn. That's it.

This means you must discriminate, and not on any racial, religious, or gender grounds. But rather, on who you want to work with, and who you don't.

Listen, once you've written a book, what you're really doing is increasing demand for you and your products and services. You see, many years ago I would accept clients paying me about $100 per hour, but now that I've written 10 books, and run additional businesses, there's much more demand for me, and my time, experience, and knowledge.

And while the supply of me has remained constant, this obviously translates into being able to command substantially higher prices. Not demand, but command and have people virtually standing in line to work with me.

Time is money! Period! I'm not suggesting you don't respond to fan mail, but be smart about your investment of time. The folks that feel entitled to your time, don't go to work for free, so neither should you! You're not your brothers keeper, and it's good to want to help him. But you can't live someone else's life for them. And one of the best ways to help other people, is often to help yourself first! This is how Bill Gates is able to change the world with his charitable acts. By first helping himself, earn more resources to achieve this noble goal.

There's a few strategies to deploy to engineer your business, to meet your needs, wants, and desires. And one of the most beneficial is to hire a gatekeeper.

You see, within my industry being inaccessible makes me even more attractive to wealth. And I prefer to work with a waiting list of people, eager to access me in exchange for their gold. It's been a pleasant surprise to discover the less accessible I am, the more demand there seems to be.

A colleague of ours, compares this principle to sleeping with a guy on a first date. Now I personally, won't accept anyones unscheduled phone calls, or instant communication. Even from people wanting to give me their gold, they've got to wait before they'll get a response. Instant communication is blasphemous to wealth attraction!

All my communications get funneled through my gatekeeper Lauren. She screens out the majority of the time vampires, and entitled people, so I don't ever have to see them. And believe me, it's worth it! If you're the money man in your business, you must invest your time in activities that produce gold. After all, this is your business and you should engineer it to meet your desires, wishes, and preferences.

It boggles the mind to see people using a so called smart phone in the restroom, and taking client phone calls in the airport. Look, if my call is of such little importance to you, that you'll accept it when you're standing at the urinal, you're not someone I'm interested in doing business with. And if your business is so replaceable, that you have to answer a phone call or else you'll lose a customer to the next business in the phone book. You've got some serious work to do my friend.

You see, even when you're being paid big money per hour, people will still ineffectively use your time. Just last week, I was talking with a client, whose paying me hundreds of dollars per hour. And the first thing he said during our session, planned weeks in advance, was can you hold on a minute. Sure, but only because you've already paid and the checks cleared.

This brings me right along to the next point, get paid in advance. You see, it's easy to turn away clients, and money, when you have a list of people eager to pay you weeks, even months in advance. And at just about any price you ask. When you're desperate to make a sale, and need money, you have no position of power, no way to negotiate. The sale is only based upon price.

It's wise to create a list of characteristics that clients must meet, in order to work with you. It's also good to have a minimum. You see, people will reach out to you wanting to create partnerships, but just because you can earn money with something, doesn't demand that you should invest your time with it.

For me, if a project doesn't meet my minimum, I'll turn it down in a flash. My time is money, and so is your's, especially if you're a producer in this world, rather than another one of the many takers.

You'll discover what best suits you and your business with experience. At the end of the day, remember this is your business. You don't have to accept any ole random persons, communication, money, or demands! And one of the best ways to discover your preferences, is to make some mistakes. For I could share an endless number of stories, where I made bad, and very costly decisions! Now the key is to learn something from those situations, so you don't repeat the same mistakes.

Dan Moskel

Chapter 18. Change The World

Hear my testimony I owe my life to a book. For when I was a boy of only 12 years old, I had a brain aneurysm rupture. Naturally, this left my parents in deep despair, worry, and filled with anxiety.

We talked with a number of surgeons and the outlook for my future, even with a successful operation without complications was dim, to put it mildly. Only through a book that a member of my dad's church discovered, did we learn about Dr. L. Nelson Hopkins, in Buffalo NY. We immediately visited Dr. Hopkins, and decided he was the right man for me.

And thank God, because during my brain surgery everything went wrong! My aneurysm burst again, and the surgery lasted nearly 15 hours. Afterwards I spent four days in an artificial coma, and upon awakening I'd lost the ability to communicate. I couldn't talk, walk, write, read, nothing. My life was over as I knew it!

Vividly do I recall, one afternoon in the I.C.U when I couldn't communicate to my dad or the nurses, that I had to pee. And in a moment of defeat did I lay upon my bed, and urinate on myself. To this day one of the most humbling experiences of my life.

A few weeks later only through what can be called a miracle of all miracles, did I have a grand mal seizure, and was instantly restored with these precious gifts of communication! How fortunate, lucky, and grateful I am to be alive and talking with you today!

This was all the result of a book! And while I'd like to say this was my biggest challenge in life, it certainly is far from the only obstacles. For Dale Carnegie, again, saved my life having attended five different high schools. His words and lessons contained in his famous book *How To Win Friends and Influence People* showed me a way to make these transitions far easier.

You see, your book, no matter the topic or genre has the power to save someone's life. To give them hope, encouragement, and transform their future.

Build Your Legacy of Greatness

Now, I hope it's safe to say you've created your books to help other people, build a legacy, and help yourself earn the best kind of gold. The passive, recurring income.

The big key is you must act on the material contained within these pages. Don't just think positively about it, do it! For action is one trait, all successful people have in common. You must act, and act right now! And inaction is a decision by default!

Banish the false belief of a four hour work week. For Winston Churchill said it best with: *"Continuous effort not strength or intelligence is the key to unlocking our potential."*

Please, use this material. It's application is universal and when you become skilled at selling, you're cultivating one of the most difficult skills. Thus, the most valuable skill.

For bringing people in the door, is the only way businesses are run. And thanks to the internet, that metaphorical door now extends online, and world wide.

Free Gift From The Author - Dan Moskel

Now because we're committed to your book marketing success, if you've yet to visit DanMoskelUniversity.com and sign up for your free bonus gifts, which include a training course with videos to see behind the scenes and how exactly to most effectively use these marketing weapons. And you'll be getting an invitation to attend up coming live copywriting event.

And for the first 100 people that visit DanMoskelUniversity.com and join our congregation, you'll get two more bonuses with a retail value of $197.00. The first is a review of your book description page, the sales letter. And the second is a free media interview, with me, to create the first of your automatic sales funnels, for your book!

And we have so much more we need to share with you. If you're one of the few, brave, courageous entrepreneurs that's ready, willing, and dedicated to getting addicted to earning money, visit our website and sign up. For more about Dan, and information about consulting, speaking engagements, copywriting assignments, details are available at DanMoskelUniversity.com.

You can also contact Dan at:

dmoskel@gmail.com
803.422.5795

Other Books by Dan Moskel

- *How To Write a Book - The System*

- *Video Marketing For Entrepreneurs*

- *Email Marketing That Works ... So You Don't Have To*

- *The Magical Message of Success*

- *How To Create a Website Easy Button: Earn Money Online with Google AdSense, Amazon, Your Business, and More*

- *SEO Training Manual - The 10 Golden Steps To Shower In Search Engine Traffic*

- *Entrepreneur Bible To Riches*

- *The Blueprint to Affiliate Marketing: Revealed My Exact Million Dollar Earning Strategies, Tips, and Tricks*

- *Online Marketing - The Shark Attack*

www.ingramcontent.com/pod-product-compliance
Lightning Source LLC
Chambersburg PA
CBHW051807170526
45167CB00005B/1919